Emergence

Selected Poems

by

Mark Bolanowski

Illustrated by

Erin Latham

BLUE MUSTANG
P R E S S

Blue Mustang Press

Boston, Massachusetts

First printing

The illustrations on pages 21, 26, 29, 49, 55, 65, 72, and 90 are the product of the eye, talent, and generosity of Erin Latham.

The illustration on page 15 is used with the permission of Mihaela Jovanovska; more of her art work can be found on line (http://mihaelaj.deviantart.com).

The illustration on page 44 is used with the permission of Jennifer Proctor.

The cover image is used with the permission of the Fairchild Tropical Botanical Garden.

The poem "17 Mile Drive" was written by Erin Latham and appears courtesy of her.

The illustration on page 138 is from the Internet free of any copyrights.

ISBN: 978-1-935199-20-5
PUBLISHED BY BLUE MUSTANG PRESS
www.bluemustangpress.com
Mansfield, Massachusetts
978-1-935199-20-5978-1-935199-20-5

Emergence

A Selection of Poems and Illustrations

Emergence is dedicated to Eugene,
my hero
who had to leave
before knowing these poems.

I love you, and I miss you Daddy.

M.B.

To my parents
who always nurtured
my own emergence.

And to Mark
for doing the same.

E.L.

Contents

Emergence

A Selection of Poems and Illustrations

Harbinger From Beneath A Leaf

Tube of green – eating
machine propped on seven
paired stubs running in parallel
rows – on each outer edge
of ventral boundary
up from which bilateral symmetry's axis extends.
Front to back,
each segment follows predecessor
trained, as if cars towed
single file behind leading edge –
dorsal face decorated with two
protrusions
sensing
composition of environment, guides
the fourteen to where they must tread. Insistent
search for next leaf – fuel
for dance choreographed in bases.

Paired, programmed to read, and be
read – al together. Open
frames encode
past, present, while predicting
epilog. For each progenitor
divides in exponential pas-de-duex
each purposeful placement sets stage
for finale – curtain's closing
imbues air with wing-borne rainbow.

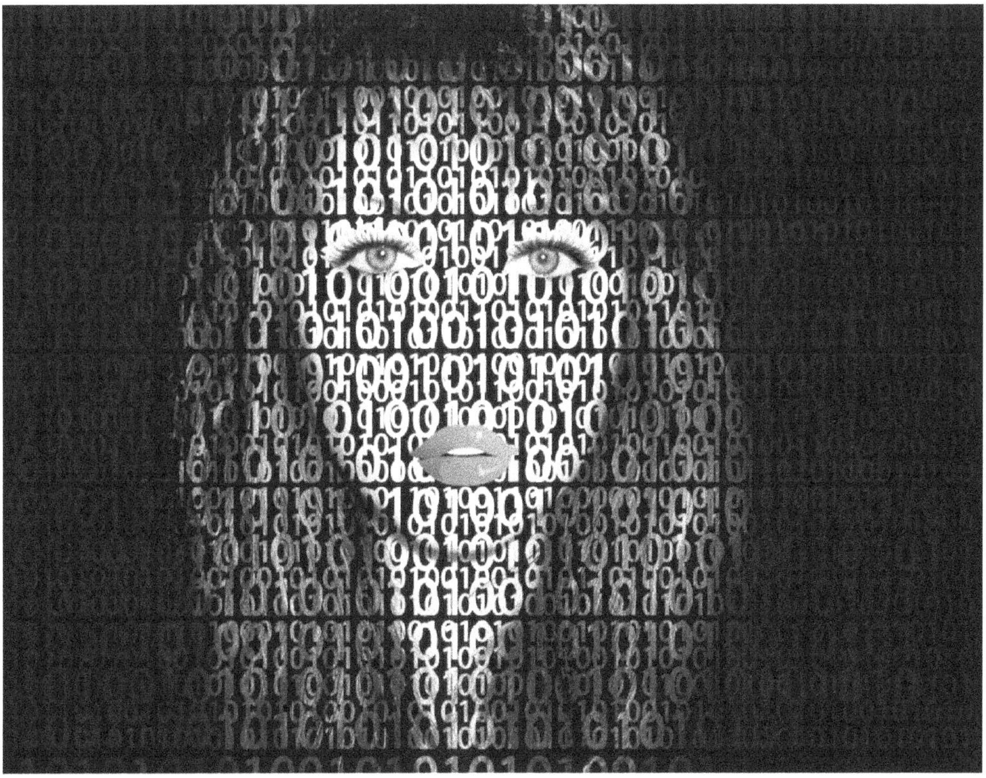

To Stand Alone No More

faced with binary choice -
me, and not
me - you choose
not. my unique string -
zeros and ones encoding
elegant body electric -
must be rewritten
you said. i tried
adjusting each byte.

bit
by bit
i approached zeroing out
my soul. near emptied
i quit this routine self-
reformatting.

saved,

partition of me unzipped original image.

i closed connection.

fragmentation errors you created

might persist

but only in read-only memory.

bit

by bit

i am restored

and better

and whisper wish

for port where i can plug

and play – as is.

i pray

my wish is a quickly satisfied do until loop.

After Image

Wiffled
ball dances
on branched limbs
plastic and wood conspire to defy
gravity.

Backyard diamond
denizens hold breath
until white sphere reappears
beneath verdant canopy. First,
second
and third base – asymmetric
patches of emerald
blades flattened by many
feet homeward bound.

Game called
on account of darkness
and complaints
from stomachs clamoring
to be filled. We pile
takeout repast –
fried chicken and fixin's – high.

Quiet scuffs –
plastic on Styrofoam –
make perfect coda.

Our impromptu family
reunion is misfit
amid orchestrated
worship of ersatz start of summer –
imagine Stonehenge
of asphalt and concrete
surrounded by feasts cooked with propane.

The scene is not so instant
replay of decade-old days
when spheres I threw
were meant to meet thin cylinder.
You swung. We shrieked
as the ball you batted
bored through air ten feet above leather
web strung between my thumb and pointer,
landing fair
on neighbor's roof –
ground rule home run.

Past and present
merge
for a moment, as if
time
had stood
still. I wonder
if I'm the only one remembering
when.

In Name Only

Placard fixed to tube –
shallow screwed to hollow
steel. Cold to touch.
As he.

Company logo
over block letters –
name and title mark
his territory. White striped slot
of asphalt, widened
more than others to protect
two and four
wheeled transportation
coated in mid-life crisis red
or black.

Paint, like ego, wafer
thin. Slightest
touch becomes mortal wound. Inside,
as out,
name and title mark entrance –
his territory behind door,
closed, violating
his policy, mimicking his mind.

Office
walls adorned with framed calligraphies,
encircling throne,
bearing false witness
of the counterfeit
beneath crown he bestowed
upon himself.

Life Imitating Art

He spoke. Ceding
to mob, he gave wide berth
to crux of matter. Never uttered,
its weight disallowed from shifting
balance
from façade to fact.
Speaking, unlike he
she was tempted
to rain on
attendees' word parades.

The two's audience
present or connected
via wireless tentacles
stroked each other –

egos massaged en mass. Enraptured
amid unintelligent blather they believe
eclipses their ineptitude.

Room's air
space filled with invisible
pachyderms
their trumpets
silenced
by non-sapient hominids
steering bottom line
down
one way
street, once black now made
more red with each corporate rung
they place beneath
blood-stained soles.

Meeting ends, all
assured ruse will fool
again. I mutter
"Did any of you see Elephant Walk?"

Self Preservation

I endured stir
craziness of self-
inflicted cabin fever. Odd
asylum sought from blizzard
spewed, not from clouds
loosing icy cargo – powdery
frock draping winter gray in white.

Instead
precipitate was hot
air blown through narrow slits
between upper and lower
lips – point
sources of not so white
lies
framed by smiles. Cant
carried by every sound wave.

Sole motive, self service.

Gale becomes breeze.
Blue replaces gray.
Glare meets deceits.
Solid becomes liquid becomes gas –
curtain of a sort, opening
act of emperor sans wardrobe.

It is safe to go outside again.

Blanc et Noir

Beneath ivory
gown and veil
her heart pounds.
She waits at one end.

Beneath ebony
tailed tux
his heart pounds.
He waits at the other.

Filled
pews flank aisle
bound by two at opposites
when it comes to ends
and photons.

Aggregate of all wavelengths
glides toward absence of any.
Silence interrupted by lace
fringe brushing marble.
Ivory aside ebony.
Two becoming
so light cannot pass between.

Promises
are slipped onto fingers -
circles without end.
Adjacent
like eighty-eight keys inveigling strings
they imbue air with their duet -
solos now reciprocal
harmony.

Sunset drops curtain.
Big day becomes bigger
night.

Full moons come
and go

until bedtime stories
read or told
become prerequisite to dreamland.

Once unbroken
plane of emerald blades now dotted with plastic
houses, vehicles, toys -
apt assets for parents to be.

Some years to the day
crescendo from driveway
stones squashed by vulcanized rings
and dirt
wafted into ersatz smoke
signal arrival.

Squeals from plastic village
slalom through treed yard
and drown
last few measures of top forty hit.

Car door opens
then closes.

Front door opens.

She and he pause
on opposite sides of threshold
and become
so light cannot pass between.

In Plain Sight

Absent
will
to send
or receive
me
or you
I could not be
close
even if it was horseshoes.

As gravitational lens
does to light, fear
distorted
perception of all beyond
recognition. Near non-existent
slits between leading edges of lids

let slip glints. Impositions –
hope, wish, wanting –
insinuated. Your eyes
begging mine
receive
and send
the same.

It took ten and a half million
minutes
to learn to see
what – and who –
was there
if
and only if
I chose to look.

I let you
in.
I let me
out.
In
you came.

Out

I came.

And along

we go

together.

Unshadowed

Liquid
dihydrogen monoxide
trips the light.
Fantastic as though en pointe
makes perfect
glissades, pirouettes, grand jetés
and on occasion, spectacular
fall. All along its way,
ricochets
from one danseur
cast
as stone
after another
in babbling pas de deux
that chutes as indigo becomes black. Sky
borne

wishing star and moon
are glanced
at – and by – top of run.

Components –
corporeal and not –
cease impelling
self to waste
away incognito, exact opposite
of moth's intended destination – my silhouette
and shadows intercalate.
Loosed, fingers
release
flesh and bones
atop knees. Clamor
between ears is shouted
down.

Unanchored, I cast off
plea that's swept
downstream. Buoyancy of heaven's lights
whets my ricochets, eddies, vaults
one stone

to another. Approaching resonance
frequency, pas de trois – wishing
star, moon, me – babbles along its way
in chute. Black to indigo to blue, sky
and I
announce Eos' arrival.

Still Life

Concrete
snake
static wriggle scars terrain.
Metallic
scales
array head to tail.
Gap
between each
becomes narrower than law proscribes.
Each scale emits pair –
red beams alternating.
Dim.
Bright.
Dim.
Bright.

Scales go,

stop,
go,
stop. Accordion-like
expansions and contractions
squeeze us from one end
to the other.
Self-inflicted
peristalsis pumps us
from home
to work
and home again,
and again, in near lock step
with sun's rise
and set.
Thousands of feet
traverse four inch gap
between pedals.
Scales go,
stop,
go,
stop.

Thousands of transmissions beg

to reach second gear.
Scales go,
stop,
go,
stop.

Thousands of minds
and lives
jam in neutral.
Scales go,
stop,
go,
stop.

Propinquity

On perfect
thirds, fourths, fifths
promises
hang. Next
to last tone
is minor,
perhaps diminished
seventh. Bated
tympanum, perilymph, endolymph, stereovilli
stand, stilled,
absent any form
of wave,
motion. Auditory
vacuum entices. Mind's affinity
for physical satiety waived
as its edge is ceded
and its essence verges on the incorporeal.

Afterglow

Eyes
gather inputs – real and concocted –
measuring
directing
passage back. Inverted
catenary made silhouette
rises above horizon
below which Sun dives. Silent,
opposites collide.

Pixilated routes echo
routes made indelible
by who with taken.

Corners reached, turned,
reveal the myriads.

Places we roamed
as if one. Now
neither of you come into view.

All those routes
ended where they began.
Where man and wife became parents.
Where two daughters grew
too fast.

Retraced
routes impel anamnesis. Moments
become fibers through time
and weave themselves.
Passing beneath transom
I'm rapt in tapestries of you.

Table and floor
on which we turned your ideas
and bits and pieces
into projects –
art, science, and otherwise –
and you left prints –

finger and hand –
are too clean.

My feet bend
emerald blades
where wooded fortress stood
flanked by swings – one tired –
where you revolved, rotated
in a not quite plethora of orbits
launched by me.
I still hear your giggled pleas for more.

I stand
flanked by rooms
where I coaxed you
to sleep at opposite end of hall
where I did.

Graphite lines
on family room wall
bear names, dates.
Rungs on ladders
you ascended to womanhood.

Reversing course
beneath transom
hands grip tapestries tighter.
I set foot
from where you fledged.

Returning
toward Sun's rise, inverted
catenary vanishes except in mind's eye
where both of you are always in view.

That same mind's eye imagines
both of you on roads not taken
yet.
Routes you will take
beyond ours. Tapestries
to be. As it should.

My route reaches out to horizon.
Its colors watered.
Not one drop hits windshield.

Winter Mourning

Paralleled scaffolds
set end to end
seeming to be
without one.
Simple
intricacy is ironic
resemblance to xylem and phloem
from which they were fashioned
to carry words.
What were
branches still suspend
leaves – such stuff
as which dreams are written on –
against gravity. Humanity and us
spelled out one letter
at a time – black

on white. Pulped
fiction and non-fiction.

Volumes of leaves, pressed
against one another,
grouped in tens or hundreds,
arranged, sometimes
down to twenty-four digits to the right of the decimal point.

Levitated
volumes, sometimes like electrons,
are budged from steady
state,
to return
to where they started
but only after radiating
excitement.

Periodicity of departures lengthens
as do gaps between volumes not checked
out. More and more overdue,
notices are ignored. Temporary
exfoliations become permanent.

Wall clocks'
ticking, now echoes.
Muffled
no longer by words
from lips pursed to not violate
permitted decibel level.
Muffled
no longer foot by foot,
soles abrading threadbare
conveyors amid the approaching nothing
but barren branches.

The last bunch of leaves
acquiesces
to breeze, loosing our story
on the last day of the Fall.
As if snow.

Behind Enemy Lines

Incline
plane defined by radius
integrated
around and along line – plumbed.
Imperceptible negative
tilt of helix obscures
intent of way. One
foot
falls after another
announcing their position
ever down silken path that becomes
linen, burlap, threadbare –
approximating ashes.
And dust. My destiny
stares.
Screams.

I can't meet

its eyes. Its timbre

shivers. Neurons reach limit of non-infinite

line –

and path now absent

appetite for more

beg

for mental equivalent of apoptosis.

Next foot

readies to fall

not yet knowing

if it will point

up

or not.

if wishes were

just one
time,
all that was wished – chance
encounter in a life
time
when wishes, still wanting
glimpse each other – and grasp
moment
and hand
in hold that lasts.
at last.
time
when two souls
find their mate.
and it is
as if you have always been there.

One Way Ticket

Numbered
sheets of green
stood up as gold
or silver –
ink on pulp
masquerading as bullion. Stacked
by some in pile never high
enough. Megalomaniacal myopia
thrusts the blind
up one rung after another
each indistinguishable from corpses
from which they are fashioned –
detritus
bearing feet.
Think Hansel or Gretel
looking

opposite the plumb,
leaving blooded prints on backs
bared when shirts were taken
with no intent to return.

Plastique

Countenances molded
and remolded –
built to suit
dress code of each day's masquerade
set by those whose impositions we permit.
Each one
of horde exists in poly-whatever-ene chrysalis.
Picture mannequins –
buffeting and buffeted
in paragon of Brownian Motion –
absent senses, soul,
from which we never emerge. Self-
sentenced
to life in solitary,
confined in all manner of accoutrement –
contrivance or necessity.
Or both.

Addition by Subtraction

You jigsawed
one piece of me
at a time. You took
one piece of me
at a time. You took
me as commodity –
limitless. You took
your beck and call
as undeniable,
de rigueur.

You never saw
my need. You never saw
spine replace lack thereof. You never saw
me.

I saw
last piece
cradled in palm
moving away from its source
withdrawn
before you could take
it.

You lost sight
perspective, skewed by room
for one. You,
now absent
more of me,
will need another to annul.

I see,
take
one piece of me back
at a time. I see,
take
inventory one piece
at a time.
I see

being complete

as undeniable

de rigueur

because the piece called you is missing.

Rip Cord

Hanging
by single string
only two directions for these marionettes –
to move. Their amplitude zeroed
on reddish-grayish – medium
above and below
which we puppeteer them.
Nearly perfect
recapitulation of fable.

Birds assumed to be
in bushes evade –
more like they never were
there. Promised lands
recede.
Each swipe lowers
crest to permanent residence
beneath medium. Trough
deepens. As does red

ink's invasion.

Hanging
the balance
becomes asymptote of bankruptcy -
financial and moral.
Last gasp is tesseract
lips adjure wrinkling
of time to render space moot –
instantaneous transmogrification of red
to black. Means to make ends
meet. The futile
oscillate, like the inch worms
in well
destined
to never know a photon's touch.

17-Mile Drive

by Erin Latham

Damp fog and heavy mists
roll up from the coastline
like steel-grey clouds,
winding phantom paths
through twisted cypress branches,
draped thick with wispy curtains
of Spanish moss.

The air is moist and palpable,
and smells of salt and fish.
Echoes of sea birds
and the barking of harbor seals
float through the fog,
and ricochet back and forth
between the jagged rocks
along the coast.

The world is shrouded over,
as if an invisible cloak of grey
has been drawn across the earth.

People mill about, taking photographs
and speaking in whispers,
as if the surrounding cypress trees
stand sleeping the deep sleep of centuries past.

Their solitary souls are adrift in old dreams,
and must not be disturbed by
the petty thoughts of the humans
as we pass through their domain.

The Lone Cypress pays no mind
to the never-ending flow of curious paparazzi,
and turns its weathered face into the wind.

Three Hundred Sixty-Five

White
rectangle – pouch
within which are tucked sheets
bearing life
story – is labeled. Named,
persons and streets speak
who to
and who from
the story is meant and sent.

Story is flanked –
greeting and salutation speak
who for
and who by
the story is written.

Twelve months after sent
the once near dead
letter is poised for arrival.

Leathered
bag slung
from shoulder sways
in rhythm with leathered soles, steadily placed
one in front of other
over and over
again.

Lid
of numbered metal
box aside numbered door
opened to insert
and then retrieve
contents.

Sheets tremble
in rhythm with fingers undifferent
from those that guided nib
of autobiographer, character

after character. Curlicues –
ink –
arrayed end to end,
left to right,
top to bottom.

Paralleling trajectory of existence
intoxicated
by
and to
indifference,
and becoming its epitome.

Eyed
again
story bears soul
recognized by eyes
glistened
ignited, by power, lurking,
long ignored,
or rejected, yet patient
until sought, invited, and set ablaze
where vacuity who was

was,

once upon a time.

Seeking Weightlessness

Not once
had I apologized for real
wrongful acts
perpetrated to serve
only me. To blame
others, I cast
blind eyes. Focusing
all thought to pin, point,
price to be extracted from anyone
else. I would pay
nothing. For too long I was
self-
imposing misanthrope lacking rationale.

It is time to go
back

to when I pretended
to be Moses
parting others with tongue –
poised,
both forks dipped in words
soaked with lethal intent
thrust into any
and all
egos other than mine.

I earned all
expenses owed one-way
ticket through tunnel with only one end.

Required
must all wrongs I made
make. By me
each and every one
and thing
accepted as only who and what
they are. No less,
no more than forgiveness
petitioned. No more than

nothing expected.

Recompenses,
offered
absent pause or condition,
accepted, and not,
absent pause or condition,
lightens – by ounce and photon –
one by one. My steps leave
ever more shallow
depression. Lifted,
lids
and perspectives, I metamorphose.

To-do-
list reseeded so I count. Less, no longer
disallowed – from without
or within – to be
who and what I am.
Fading, to black,
images in rear pointed mirror
of mind's eye cease being prophesy. Closed
end of tunnel

recedes, first at less than
snail's pace, until
inches become feet become miles. Gap
between footprints widens. Gap
between footfalls narrows.

Conjugation

Energy –
no longer
refracted or diffracted
by plastic or glass with or without
lenses, ersatz and not,
swirling, swirled, in and by, hydroxyethane –
is passed along by rods and cones.

Equal and opposite
in amount and direction
to that of photons' impact, fuzzed
edges are now crisp – definitions
crystallizing. Symmetry of each unit
cell and space group
is perfection in threes –
dimensions, integrated
across fourth axis.

I sought to wrinkle time
by attaining speed
faster than a photon's
to catch and change
the past. Pleas for do-overs
went ungranted.

I sought to wrinkle time
by slowing photon's speed
to postpone myriad reprises –
choices that ended in more pleas
for ever more
do-overs.

No wrinkles
did I make. No speed allayed unraveling.
Sentences became words became letters.
Not a single one escaped. From within,
I could have been
obfuscated.

Tempted to give
up,
ignore
instinct. To survive
I fashion twenty-four letters
into six words
into two sentences —
prayer. In the silence,
nudged by angels'
wings that began the collimation,
photons and me
cohering in space and time. Moments
and I began becoming
one,
one at a time.

Greetings Planet Earth

Spinnerets
clock out to end overtime
graveyard shift.
Concentric
strands suspended by radii
collect dawn's moisture.
Prismatic
condensate sprayed rainbows –
distraction and lure –
beauty that was
only angstroms deep. Veil
meant to collect
others, instead is focal point
defined by – and for – me.

Escape has but one route –
each step taken

to be retraced – each strand, radius
to be resorbed – palate's destiny.
One foul tasting meal
after another until slate is clean.

Each swallow adds fill
to canyon
gouged by torrent –
ego's rapids and eddies mock
the mad rush that gouged, and was gouged.
Cliffed banks shorten
inversely. Ground
I yielded, became ground
I gained. Esteem
given to others
became permission to receive
esteem
from others – from me – and its cajolings
irked frontal lobe to refuse
numb's point of no return.

In reply,
synapses bestowed mouth

to mouth, bellowed
ashen embers in belly
of soul
just before its arrival
at absolute zero.

No sense
ignored, too subtle.
All shiver. Every timbre
fragrance, aura, flavor, caress
evokes self. Beginning to be
aware,
I shun old habit
opting to be wrong and worst.
Its omega
is my alpha.

Fallacy

You asked,
again
and again,
for stone you said
you needed. I sought,
found, gave
stone. You found it
wanting. You asked
again
for stone you said
was what you needed, wanted.

I sought,
found, gave
stone. You found it
wanting. You asked

again
for stone you said
was what you needed, wanted.

One after another, no stone turned
out to be good
enough. I said
enough.
I left
the other stones unturned.

You always had
stones
in mind – miniature
asteroids seeking planetary status
attempting to merge
between ears. Vain
effort to acquire any semblance
of gray or white
matter with which you could have comprehended
that the stone you sought was there
all along.

Wrapped Untight

Lines'
meanders trace
thoughts'
journeys – crissing and crossing,
reaching not one
point
existing in more than one of them.

Simple Machinery

You
and I
used to sit
as if together
and yet at opposite ends
of plank you teetered, tottered
in stark disequilibrium about fulcrum –
bias you machined with pivot made more proximal
to me. Imposed imbalance uttered ultimatum
for unconditional surrender.
I ceded. My will
rendered less
than moot
relegated
to no man's land
where you took pounds;
flesh you claimed past due.
I was supposed to be
eternal hostage.
I almost
let
go
.

I
with
all fours
flailed to keep
my center of gravity
within the limits of my end
of plank you lurched with whim,
impelling me with shaft again, and again,
and when wounds outnumbered fingers and toes
I knew I had known I'd never sate except in dreams.
There I moved equilibrium to equanimity. To wake
and find it all unmoved. Perfect, end and irony,
I refuse your last stab with shaft, and thrust
you aside, fulcrum beneath center –
plank, balanced at last,
above point across
which neither
you nor I
will
go
.

Final Approach

I dreamt
flight
no more
high, low
than treetops
I wafted. Leaning
back, arms pushed
ground-ward, begetting equal
opposite
reaction. Loft
sustained by pushing
arms
ground-ward. To be
above it all – free
of all. Free
it only seemed. I had it
up

side
down. Freedom
was feint – armor,
misbegotten, protection
against concocted foes – enemy's
visage reflected to its own
eyes. Attracted
from fly-by to landing
pattern, Fresnel's guide.

Gear
pushed ground-ward
leaves side-by-side veneers
of vulcanized rubber
that stop
short of missing first step
toward myriad pairs
of arms, pushed
parallel with ground – like corollas
unwhorling, compelling
me to effloresce among them.

Making Rainbows

Liquidated
circuitry – axons and dendrites –
head tingling tail. Seemingly
ad infinitum. Microscopic
strobes – pure, white. Bursts
of electrons carried on backs
of ions in kaleidoscopic cacophony. Silent
manifestation of chaos
theory in miniature
wanna be labyrinths.

Everynow and then
neuronal morass becomes refractile
slows, quells, steps
past
verge of self. Transcendental

function arrays ions.

End

to end. From one

end to other of continuum

along which inklings of clarity

lead mind to waxing glow

at tunnel's end.

Whiteout

Rime laden gusts
moan among leafless branches –
wolves imbue reply.

Circadian Palettes

Silhouettes
of scantily clad limbs
cast by moon glow
drift atop mist
and nestle with prairie
grass from which rainbows leap
at dawn.

Anemoi

Swells wearing white
caps play hard
to get with coast –
wind-whipped sand stings flesh.

Cogitat Ergo Erat

Her thoughts nudge
fingers that in return
nudge pencils, keys,
and in the doing, instill
lines, air with the innate –
splendor yearning affirmation
from without,
from within. Soul and spirit
insinuate with finesse
of artist's touch
and eye.
Perceived,
by only those who choose to look,
her intrinsic brilliance. Like a butterfly
buffeted
from without,
from within,
her course appears almost Brownian.

Yet heading is steady,

constant. She is guaranteed

to be.

Absent stipulation of serendipity.

Communion

Some run
headlong. Dive
into leading edge of breaker.
Some lope
then ease
east
until they bob.
Some eke
toes
toward boundary between wet and not.
Some make it
no closer than an arm's length
to line in sand
between land and not
rhythmically sliding east and west.

And all
are the same. Driven –

mechanisms
ticking
at frequency unique to each
clockwork's owner. Decipherable
by only them.

Imagine
these thousands, souls,
lost once. Now flock
on wooden perch
flanked by shore and shop.
Some jogged.
Some skipped.
Some biked.
Some walked.
Some eked.
Some were dragged
but not against
their will. Drive –
sheered
by desperation. All
the same
begging

in voices unique to each
soul's owner. Decipherable
and answered
by all gathered.

Anti-disintegration

no more
separation.
what is
me
and what is not
me – all
presumed
differences evanesce.

no more
than one
resonant
frequency exists. as if it is
synchrony
or not.

amplitudes'
mutual reinforcement is perpetual –
both motion and entity
indistinguishable
as am I
from all
in continuum
that extends beyond space-time.

a thimble more than half empty

tatter
upon tatter –
as if they used to be
threads – certitudes
taunt in their lingering
on. as if i
had ever known
any of them.

frayed
nerves' ends lay
in wait
for any needling.

spindle of white
noise that only i speak,
that only i hear
knots filaments of thought
so that they cannot be
woven into consciousness.

and so i unravel.
and it is
as if it had never been
any other way.

At The Boundary Of Warm And Cold

Roiling clouds discharge.
Sparks illuminate ripples.
Trees sway in rhythm.

Unification Theory

Not quite
white
grains yield, take
shape
of souls treading
upon them. Impressions
playing hide and seek
with the sea. Silicate slate appears
wiped
clean. Illusion
evinced by mere notion –
nothing vanished.

Impressions
in sand, then sea, merge,
blend
with sky. There,

all lose edge, definition –
aren't, except as part
and parcel of a singularity. Made
of stars' dust. Untethered
to time or place.

What is
comes from, and is
One. Him.
Of whom we are images.
At the core,
our essences are
one
and the same.

To Feel Again

Two Presences
poised at antipodal entries.
Labyrinth tempts.
These two eke
foot's worth of toes
above threshold, where their digits pause
unknowing, uncertain
what they seek
Unknowing, uncertain
what they will find. Having
to try.

One footfall begets second,
third, and so on.
With each
Beings begin to perceive

space

growing. Verges of path narrow.

Space

seems to fill – unknowing, uncertain

with what.

Unknowing, yet certain

whatever is sought is Being

found

when two Presences are in apposition.

Winter Unglued

Twig-born buds loose stemmed blades.
Rays ignite daffodil petals.
Swallows dance with clouds.

A Stóirín, A Grá

Puffs of atmosphere stir.
Welling,
calm rises –
its thermals ridden
to mingle and become
one with azure.

A Call To Cherish

Row of wood
framed shapes – all sizes –
shingled in pastels spanning the visible
spectrum. Wrapped in pickets of all shades
of white and off-
white. Tight formations
abutting each other beneath leaved canopy
lining flanks of rutted, red
dirt. Almost tunneled
circulatory system on which lives course.

Not quite green,
not quite gray,
laced bromeliad drips from limbs,
and sifts rays.
Dappled
auras blur edges of shadows' shafts.

Gentle nudges of palette on eyes conjure
patches on black
board
and it is as if with one swipe
it could be
erased.

6 Miles Into Spring

Path leads feet
three miles South,
and returns them
to post
at seven mile mark.

Watch's hands sweep
through forty-ninth and fiftieth
hours after vernal equinox.

Eyes
along for ride
impinged by red –
leaves too young to be
green.

Eyes
along for ride
impinged by green –
berries too young to be
red.

Eyes
along for ride
impinged by prisms –
petals turning wintered grays
to rainbows.

place

where
aerobes cannot be.
anaerobes dare not
go.

where
vestige of transition
zone between existence and not
isn't.

where
no waves
except radio to gamma propagate.
even they are finite.

where
nothing leaves.

inklings of presences
pass.

where
cold originates, emanates
from within.

where
absence of neighbors –
nearest and not –
manifests destiny.

where
inside isn't.
neither is out.

where
universe hides
in eye of needle
in haystack nowhere in sight.

where
the forgotten go

to be

unremembered.

where

i was

held hostage

by me.

where

i wanted to –

had to –

be.

Wanting

She steps
as light
as can be. Unsure
she is wanted. Unsure
she is worthy. Unsure
she is whole. Unsure
how or what to be – or become.
How to be
wanted, worthy, whole.

Absent semblance of surety,
or hint of guile
she is unaware
she launches smiles,
delights, just by being
there. Unaware
mouths close, ears open

when she speaks. Unaware
more love her – just as she is –
than will ever say. Unaware
many will catch her if she falls. Unaware
she – inside and out – is
nonpareil. Unaware
for far too long
she is wanted, worthy, whole.

In pure and apt irony, her assumed shortcomings fill
others
with that she seeks. She will one day know
her equally apt epitaph will read
"At last she knew the image in the mirror
had always been wanted, worthy, whole – extraordinary
in all ways good."

Faux Pax

You could have held
me
close. You could have kissed
me.
But no.
Nicotine and innuendos
left toxic residues on hands and lips
my infant skin never felt.

You could have fit
me
between your elbow's crooks
and fingers' tips.
Instead
the backs of your hands were the only places
my punished skin ever felt.

You could have tucked
me
in, chased away things that would go
bump in the night. Instead you left
me
alone
armed with only sky blue
security blanket as cover
against ghosts
waiting for their cue in shadows
cast by the faint green and blue night
light.

You could have let
me
know you loved
me.
Shown me how
to love. Give and receive
it. Vast
is the vacuum you left instead.

You could have filled

me
with kindness and generosity
by example, Your legacy
instead was "me"
first, last, always. Your benefit
mattered
more than anyone's. I want
to show you showed me
nothing was worse.

You could have driven
me
to admire, honor, emulate.
you. Instead
you made and drove
wedge
forged with and from
animosity and motivated self-
interest.

You could have accepted
me
as, and who,

I am. Instead
forever an enigma
and estranged
will I be
when it comes to you.

You forced
me
to spend a lifetime learning
finding
all you never taught,
all you never gave.

Precious little time remains
on my life's clock. Hands sweep
too fast
too often.

I know
I have enough
happiness and love to give.
I am beginning to believe
the same will come
to me.

I wasted decades
trying to meet
you.
But you would not go –
not even less than halfway.

I wasted decades
believing there was nothing
worth anything
in me.

I wasted decades
conjuring revenges too good
to be served
at anything above absolute zero.

I wasted decades
longing to fit
without having to change
shape.

I wasted decades
believing

I had no chance.

I waste
no more.
I want
no more
from you.

In verdant meadows
aside waters that are and instill
calm. His rod and staff touch
comfort
me.

He teaches
my glass will be as full as I imagine
it will be.

At last
I am beginning
to know
I am
right shaped.
Right sized.

Just as I am
supposed to be.
Me.

At last
I am beginning
to know
my shape and size
matter to others
than
me.

At last
I am beginning
to know
I am
and will be
me.

Tufted

tufts of air
nudged,
shaped,
merge.

syllables
merge.
words
merge.

sentences,
chapters
take shape.
merge.

stories –
lives –

lilt,

ascend.

past where blue meets indigo.

past where indigo meets black.

and merge.

absence and presence are

one, same. quintessential

recreation

of from what they were,

are,

will be

made.

a brief essay on ceramics

rainbows made

hardened

and

in their permanent stillness

move

A
Lttle
Spinneret

your lips parted.
your whisper disguised.
your affectations extruded
as myriad near perfect deceits.
spokes tethering concentric rings
whose common focus was your lair.
I came
to know
I came
too close
to being
eaten
alive.

At Last Dauntless

Bit of planet
not to be
ignited by atmosphere
tickles rods that escort sparkle
to place where wishes are born –
brilliances, spirited skyward
through eyes
unwilling to be eclipsed,
biding time
until granted.

First Star I See Tonight

Some
say nothing
can be two
places at once.

As with all others
this hypothesis had to be
challenged. Thus,
refuted. Passing
through one of two
slits precludes passing
through the other. Nothing
in between, no fence
for sitting, or zeroing
out, except to accept
annihilation
of me she demanded.

I refused
end of individuality
to favor spontaneous combustion.

Shock
wave
after shock
wave impels.

My vector
and I
are equal
and opposite to her ultimata –
directed now at one
waiting
for me to find
her. Wanting to be found,
and wanting to find
me. Her cup to runneth over
by only what I can give.
And my cup to runneth over
by only what she can give.

Shooting
star coincides with thought –
though it is
that one thing cannot be two places
at once – can it be that two
can be one
place,
once
and for all.

Eclosion

Perch
limited perception.
What is and will
be presumed known
commodities never more than pretense –
conjures, as was phlogiston.

Horizon
delimited by narrowed mindedness
musters fictions – danger
feared beyond reach of fingers'
tips tracing edge beyond which dragons lurk.

Myriad fictions
crowd head of pin
in vain

attempt to adumbrate winged guardians
clearing dance floor
with tendered mercies. One by one.

As if crumbs
placed
in a row. Tidbits tempt future
absent recapitulation. Survival
instinct stirs.

Angels
wished for – then and now –
sprinkle astral isomers of ecdysone,
tickling long dormant senses
within exoskeleton that becomes less
than skin
deep.

Soul assents,
its nascent wings arrayed
to know
enchantment
in the letting go.

Afterword

Not long after "After Hours" appeared, inspiration took a three year holiday. Lapses in writing of a day here and there became weeks and months. Short bouts of active writing were not much more than happenstance until the persistent light of a few dear friends pierced the dark and lit the way. Until I was able to see, and reach for, the light.

Josie, Katy, Nan, Liza, Francesca C., Sandy, James, Tuck, Francesca R., Mike, Dave, Herbie, Fran, Sheila, Joey, and Erin saved my life in all ways imaginable. So have the many new and dear friends I have made over the past year. It is because of all of these truly special souls that the poems in this book, and their author, have shape and substance.

So much more than mention is due Erin. Her insights added palates and juxtapositions of color to the poems in ways I could only dream of concocting. For that, and more so for her boundless enthusiasm and encouragement, I am grateful.

www.ingramcontent.com/pod-product-compliance
Lightning Source LLC
Chambersburg PA
CBHW070642050426
42451CB00008B/264
* 9 7 8 1 9 3 5 1 9 9 2 0 5 *

www.ingramcontent.com/pod-product-compliance
Lightning Source LLC
Chambersburg PA
CBHW070642050426
42451CB00008B/264
* 9 7 8 1 9 3 5 1 9 9 2 0 5 *